THE RIGHT CAREER FOR ME

CONSTRUCTION WORKER

KATHLEEN A. KLATTE

ROSEN PUBLISHING

Published in 2025 by The Rosen Publishing Group, Inc.
2544 Clinton Street, Buffalo, NY 14224

Portions of this work were originally authored by Heather Moore Niver and published as *Careers in Construction*. All new material in this edition was authored by Kathleen A. Klatte.

Cover Designer: Michael Flynn
Intertior Designer: Rachel Rising
Editor: Kathleen Klatte

Library of Congress Cataloging-in-Publication Data

Names: Klatte, Kathleen A., author.
Title: Construction worker / Kathleen A. Klatte.
Description: [Buffalo] : Rosen Publishing, [2025] | Series: The right career for me | Includes index.
Identifiers: LCCN 2023058542 (print) | LCCN 2023058543 (ebook) | ISBN 9781499476316 (library binding) | ISBN 9781499476309 (paperback) | ISBN 9781499476323 (ebook)
Subjects: LCSH: Construction workers--Vocational guidance--Juvenile literature. | Building trades--Vocational guidance--Juvenile literature.
Classification: LCC HD8039.B89 K53 2025 (print) | LCC HD8039.B89 (ebook) | DDC 331.7/624--dc23/eng/20240226
LC record available at https://lccn.loc.gov/2023058542
LC ebook record available at https://lccn.loc.gov/2023058543

Some of the images in this book illustrate individuals who are models. The depictions do not imply actual situations or events.

Manufactured in the United States of America

CPSIA Compliance Information: Batch #CSRYA25. For further information, contact Rosen Publishing at 1-800-237-9932.

CONTENTS

INTRODUCTION

The economy runs in cycles. Sometimes everyone is prosperous; other times, money is tight. However tough times are, people still need to eat and pay bills. When you think about the sort of work you'd like to do, you need to consider a field that offers steady employment. A career in the construction industry is a solid choice.

In tough times, people might not build new houses, and municipalities might not commission big, new infrastructure projects, but things still need to be repaired. What if a furnace stops working on a freezing, snowy night? A heating and cooling specialist has to be called in to repair it so the occupants stay warm, and the pipes don't freeze and burst. If a roof leaks, roofers must come in to at least patch the problem before it becomes worse. Even at the height of the COVID-19 pandemic, when many people were out of work, outdoor construction crews were working on roadways.

Careers in construction are certainly not immune when the economy struggles. However, the variety of opportunities in the career makes it a better bet than many other industries. Society depends on construction workers to keep roads, tunnels, and bridges in good shape, which means year-round repair as well as improvements. Construction

A construction project requires many different types of professionals.

workers are responsible for building, fixing, and maintaining parks and other public areas, too. Some type of construction work goes on all year round everywhere in the world. Even when there isn't a lot of new construction, there are always renovations, such as replacing old insulation with newer, heathier, and more efficient options.

One of the things that makes construction a reliable career is that there are so many fields to choose from. They include:

- carpentry
- masonry
- plumbing
- HVAC (heating, ventilation, and air conditioning)
- electrical systems
- painting/decorating
- architectural/design

In some of these fields, you can get the necessary professional certifications in a couple years at trade school or even in an apprenticeship.

These are great options if money is tight or spending additional years in a classroom doesn't appeal to you. Others require more training or at least one college degree.

Working with plumbing or electricity often requires a license, but experience with carpentry, masonry, and painting can get you a solid job as a handyman. If you're more technically inclined, architecture or design might be a good choice. If driving large machinery seems like a good way to spend the workdays, consider a career as a crane operator or an operating engineer. Large machinery operators also maintain and repair their machines, so this can be a good option for anyone who likes tinkering with machines. Marble and tile setting work can offer room for a lot of creative design.

Whether you want to build structures that people need and appreciate, enjoy drawing and creating, or like the idea of moving massive amounts of soil and rock with a large machine, construction has plenty of options. Construction workers are valued members of the community. They make the places where we live, work, and play safe and comfortable. The following sections offer an overview of just some of the job possibilities in construction. Read on to discover construction careers to consider.

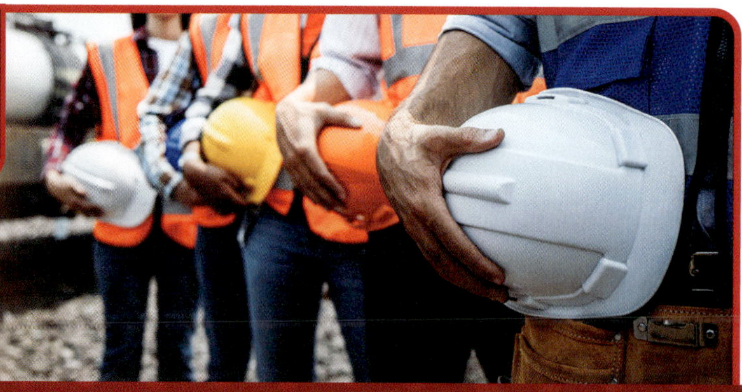

It takes many people with many different skills to complete a construction project.

HABITAT FOR HUMANITY

Habitat for Humanity is a nonprofit organization begun in the early 1970s as the Fund for Humanity. It began as a local project in rural Georgia, building safe, decent housing with volunteer labor. In 1976, it was incorporated as Habitat for Humanity International. The organization is active across the United States and around the world. Thanks to involvement by former president and Nobel laureate Jimmy Carter and his wife, Rosalynn Carter, Habitat and its activities are well known.

Habitat builds low-cost sustainable housing, provides repairs and renovations to existing homes, and responds to natural disasters such as hurricanes. The organization welcomes both unskilled laborers and licensed professionals to volunteer on its projects.

Habitat has programs for youth who are interested in community service and learning about home building. There are student-run chapters on high school and college campuses that raise funds and participate in local projects. This can be a great way to see construction projects firsthand and decide what you'd like to specialize in, all while doing good in your community.

President Carter didn't just lend his name to Habitat's Carter Work Project—he worked on building sites alongside volunteers from all walks of life.

CHAPTER ONE

ALL ABOUT CONSTRUCTION

The construction industry is complex. It's made up of many different professions. Many of these professions have their own unique systems of training and certification. For example, electricians generally train as apprentices for four to five years. In most states, they need to be licensed to work unsupervised. Electricians then have the choice to specialize in wiring new buildings, repair work, or outdoor linework (connecting buildings to the municipal electrical grid). That's a lot of choices right there!

As you consider a construction career, you need to really think about what sort of work and environment will make you happy. Indoors or outdoors? Working as part of a team, or independently? Do you want to spend a lot of time in a classroom or get right to work?

THE BUSINESS OF BUILDING

Construction is the business of building things. This includes houses and all sorts of other buildings—churches, stores, apartments, offices, schools—any sort of structure that people use. Construction workers also build roads, tunnels, bridges, dams, and retaining walls.

Construction workers also repair and renovate buildings. Sometimes plumbing, electricity, or insulation needs to be replaced to meet current building codes—or just make the building more comfortable. Some construction workers are trained to do demolition work—that is, to take a building or other structure down safely.

Whatever your job on a constructions site, safety is the most important thing. It's extremely important to wear appropriate personal protective equipment (PPE) at all times.

A construction worker includes anyone involved with work on any aspect of a structure. This includes the actual building, the pipes that bring in water and carry away waste, and the wiring that carries electricity to make lights and other appliances work. Contractors are in charge of the entire job, from overseeing the work by independent businesses, to making sure it's finished on time and within budget. Sometimes they hire subcontractors to take care of particular parts of the job, such as plumbing or electricity. Planners, drafters, architects, and engineers are all construction workers. So are carpenters, plumbers, welders, roofers, or anyone who helps a structure take shape. They create iron structures that form a building's frame or beautiful and practical tile designs to finish kitchens or bathrooms.

Any construction project requires a great deal of fetching, carrying, and cleaning up. Often these tasks fall to unskilled laborers or trainees who haven't earned their certifications. At the other end of the spectrum are architects and crew chiefs who oversee the project. These are people with degrees or professional certifications. All these different jobs come together to complete a building project.

LABORERS AND HELPERS

According to the Bureau of Labor Statistics (BLS), 1.6 million construction jobs in the United States are laborers or helpers. Often, they're considered "unskilled" workers, meaning they aren't certified or licensed in a specific area, although many have general construction knowledge and skills that help them in their job. Many high school graduates can get a job as a laborer based on their personal experiences. A labor position is a great way for young, unskilled workers to get started in the construction industry. Most construction work requires employees to be at least 18 years old, although some states such as New York allow workers at age 16 with a parent or guardian's approval.

Laborers and helpers often spend long hours outside in every kind of weather walking, climbing, crawling, and hauling. Sometimes laborers must stand for extended periods of time. These jobs can be dangerous and physically demanding. Laborers and helpers usually carry heavy tools and materials to where they're needed and clean up at the end of the day. They're often assigned repetitive tasks, such as cutting sections of lumber or pipes to specified lengths. Helpers do prep work so that higher-paid certified workers can perform their jobs more quickly.

Laborers must listen and follow directions precisely. They work with hand and power tools and help transport supplies and machinery from storage to a job site. Laborers set up scaffolding, dig ditches, clear rubble, and remove hazardous materials. Apprentices sometimes work as helpers, serving as aides to skilled workers such as carpenters and stonemasons, providing them with valuable on-the-job experience. Some laborers specialize in a specific kind of construction, while others handle more general jobs.

The average pay for helpers and laborers is about $40,000 per year, but the work is hard, dirty, and can be dangerous. Working as a laborer or helper can be a good way to see if the daily life of a construction worker is a good fit for you. It can also be a good way to see different types of construction professionals in action and decide if you'd like to specialize. Joining a union, completing an apprenticeship, and becoming licensed or certified means you earn more money. The work is also more challenging and rewarding. In some states, you can't work with plumbing or electricity unsupervised unless you're licensed.

CONSTRUCTION PROFESSIONALS

Any construction project—whether residential or commercial, indoors or out—requires countless skilled workers. Carpenters handle many kinds of jobs, including framing walls, roofing, creating molds for pouring concrete, and cabinetmaking. Stonemasons use their skills to make stone walls, steps, and floors. Electricians, plumbers, heating and cooling experts, and roofers help make homes and buildings livable. Operating engineers use heavy machinery to transport supplies, prepare land for construction, assemble cranes, and dispose of rubble and hazardous materials. Other skilled construction workers include welders, boilermakers, painters, and pile drivers.

It's possible to begin a construction career right out of high school, but most professional construction workers have additional education. Some workers complete apprenticeship or internship programs before finding entry-level positions. Some attend a vocational school or college. Skilled workers may also be expected to pursue certification. Completing an apprenticeship or training program means you earn more money than an uncertified worker. In addition, apprentices are paid for their work while training. Even if you chose construction because you like to be outdoors, don't want to spend years in a classroom, or don't have a lot of money to invest in your education, an apprenticeship is a solid option. You'll work with certified professionals on real construction projects, not just sit in a classroom. When you complete your apprenticeship, you'll earn more than unskilled workers and have no student debt.

If a specialty that requires college interests you, it's also possible to win scholarships through unions or construction-related companies such as Home Depot. Some companies will also reimburse tuition for career-related courses, provided you achieve a certain grade.

DESIGNERS

Construction projects begin on paper and computer screens, long before anyone picks up a shovel or hammer. Architects design new structures that are attractive, practical, and safe. They create the overall look of the project. Drafters prepare drawings and plans for construction workers to follow when building a structure. These are the plans that tell workers where to install the pipes, wiring, and heating, ventilation, and air conditioning (HVAC) ducts.

Surveyors determine the boundaries of property, something that needs to be recorded and verified before construction begins. Cost estimators figure out how much the entire project will cost—materials, labor, permits—everything needed to budget a project. Civil engineers design and manage the construction processes necessary for the construction of buildings, roads, bridges, and more.

Many meetings take place before construction begins. Often there are studies about how the work will impact the community.

THE IMPACT OF CONSTRUCTION

There are many factors of a proposed construction project that must be considered before any actual building begins. Some municipalities require environmental studies. Will the project require any trees to be cut down or greenspace destroyed? Will it pollute any nearby water sources? City planners want to know how much traffic a new project will attract. Can the existing roads and traffic signals handle the increase? Where will people park? Will the water mains or sewer system need to be upgraded?

People who live nearby may be concerned as well. Will there be an increase in traffic through their neighborhoods? People parking in front of their houses? Noise? Sometimes towns or cities hold public hearings so residents can ask questions about the proposed construction.

For example, a popular fast-food restaurant wants to build a restaurant near a local supermarket. There are both positive and negative factors to consider.

- It's convenient to have a fast-food restaurant nearby.
- Fast-food restaurants attract people. Strangers will come to the neighborhood.
- Restaurants generate lots of trash. Will the dumpsters attract pests? What about litter in the parking lot or in the neighborhood?
- Any business generates tax revenue for the municipality.
- How late will the restaurant be open? Will there be noise at night?
- Will the fast-food restaurant steal business from the locally owned diner or pizzeria?
- The fast-food restaurant will generate new jobs for the community.

Shop class can be a great way to get a jump on your career. Just don't forget the basics—you'll need math and science, too.

switch to a four-year school to complete your degree. Attending a local college and living at home removes the cost of travel and housing from the equation altogether. Many state universities offer a great education at a fraction of the cost of a private school.

Achieving a supervisory position might require a master's degree. However, by the time you reach that level, you might be eligible for tuition assistance or reimbursement from an employer or union.

One of the best options is a union apprenticeship. This combines classroom study with on-the-job training. Union apprentices are paid wages and benefits while they learn, so they begin their professional careers without the burden of student debt.

MEDIEVAL GUILDS AND APPRENTICESHIP

Today, apprenticeships are for adults entering the workforce. The programs usually last four or five years, and the apprentice is paid and receives benefits. Although apprenticeship has existed in some form since ancient times, modern apprenticeship has its roots in the craft guilds of medieval Europe.

In the medieval system, children were apprenticed to a master craftsman around the age of 12. An apprentice lived in the home of the master craftsman who trained them. The master was responsible for the apprentice's education and morals, such as making sure they attended church. Apprenticeship typically lasted seven years.

At the end of their training, the apprentice was known as a journeyperson. Usually, they received their own set of tools, and they were eligible to work for a master craftsman for wages. Eventually the journeyperson could establish their reputation and earn enough to open their own shop.

As trade became more industrialized, there was a greater need for unskilled labor to work in factories. The system of master and apprentice fell out of favor. However, for trades such as construction work, there really is no substitute for practical work experience.

The European system of apprenticeship extended to colonial America. If an apprentice ran away from their master, a runaway notice was posted, similar to the ads posted for runaway enslaved persons.

CHAPTER TWO

BUILDING WITH STONE

People have been building with stone for thousands of years. In fact, according to the United Nations Educational, Scientific and Cultural Organization (UNESCO), the oldest stone structure still in existence dates back to between 9,600 BCE and 8,200 BCE. The site is called Göbekli Tepe, and it's located in modern-day Anatolia. Some of the stone pillars even feature artwork that's still visible. It's amazing when you consider that this was built before computers, cranes, bulldozers, or any of the other things we consider necessary for a construction project.

Today stone is used for many purposes in buildings, from foundations that support the entire building to decorative outdoor features such as patios and walls. Careers working with stone are often readily available. Yet, like any construction job, a slow economy or bad weather can make jobs harder to find. Stonework offers options from practical work such as installing cement to more creative jobs such as designing tile.

Most stoneworkers need a high school diploma or its equivalent to start. High school classes in science, shop, math, blueprint reading, and mechanical drawing provide a great background.

Students can continue their education at a trade school or through an apprenticeship. Stoneworkers must be in good shape because they do a lot of kneeling, bending, and stretching.

The International Union of Bricklayers and Allied Craftworkers (BAC) offers apprenticeships in nine masonry specialties:

- bricklaying
- stonemasonry
- plaster
- tile laying and finishing
- marble masonry and finishing
- restoration
- terrazzo installation and finishing
- rainscreen installation
- concrete finishing

Bricklayers work carefully, so that the finished structure is level and sound.

BRICKLAYERS AND STONEMASONS

If you look out at your street, you'll see lots of brick and stonework. There are probably walls made of brick or cinderblock, houses with brick facades, and paths made of brick pavers. Bricklayers and stonemasons cut, seal, and position masonry materials. They also prepare and apply mortar. Brickmasons and block masons—or bricklayers—handle the same type of work. Brickmasons specialize in brickwork, and block masons work with cement blocks. Stonemasons build structures out of stone. They work with natural stone such as marble and granite, as well as artificial materials such as concrete. Bricklayers and stonemasons are often simply called masons.

Bricklayers use bricks and cinderblocks to create and repair numerous types of structures

Masons spend a lot of time kneeling on hard surfaces. This mason is wearing kneepads, gloves, and a hardhat to keep himself safe on the job.

such as walkways and patios. Cinderblocks are plain, heavy, and gray. They're often used to build basements or outdoor stairs—places where they either won't be seen or will be covered by other materials. Bricks are usually the familiar reddish-brown color, but they're also available in other shades of brown, tan, or gray. Workers can use bricks to build basic walls, but many people find them attractive and don't cover them with other materials. They're also used decoratively.

Bricklayers fit bricks together to create unique masonry pieces that fill all kinds of spaces. They also build walls between properties. Bricklayers sometimes create ornamental facades for houses, office buildings, and high-rises. Indoors, they create floors, walls, and fireplaces and chimneys. Block masons sometimes build walls for large structures, such as warehouses, hotels, and basements. Stonemasons work with natural and artificial stones. They build stone walls, steps, and patios outdoors, but they also create interior walls and floors.

Masons must be good at math and be able to read blueprints to bring a plan to life. This takes special training. General laborers may learn bricklaying and stonemason skills while helping trained professionals on the job. Some find apprenticeships through trade associations and masonry unions. Taking masonry courses at a technical or vocational school will increase the chances of finding a job and getting a higher starting salary. According to the BLS trained masonry workers earn an average of $50,000 to 60,000 per year.

PLASTERERS AND STUCCO MASONS

Plaster is generally used indoors. Plasterers apply it to walls, ceilings, or dividers to make them fireproof and soundproof, but it's also used as decoration. Smooth, white plaster is much nicer to look at than cinderblock. A wide flat board with a handle called a hawk holds the plaster, and workers apply the plaster with a trowel across surfaces such as concrete block, wood, masonry, or wire mesh called lath.

Molding plasterers make ornamental plaster shapes such as a doorway frame that looks like wood. Some plasterwork can be learned through long-term training on the job, but most learn through an apprenticeship program. The International Union of Bricklayers and Allied Craftworkers' International Masonry Institute includes a special certification in plaster.

Stucco exteriors are popular in hot, dry areas. Stucco is fireproof, an added benefit in places that don't get much precipitation.

Stucco is generally used outdoors. It consists of cement, white sand, and lime. Stucco masons usually use a spray gun to apply it to the outside of a building over lath, concrete, or masonry. They also apply insulation to a building's exterior. Stucco can have a decorative rough look if it contains pieces of marble or gravel. Sometimes stucco is used indoors, especially to cover a damaged wall that needs something more than a coat of paint.

NOT JUST FOR KIDS!

If you enjoy building toys, such as Lego, don't be too quick to pass them along to your younger siblings. They're actually a great way to train your mind, especially if you like to design your own projects or modify existing kits. Although you're working on a much smaller scale, you must solve a lot of the same problems as professional construction workers.

- How many tiles do I need to cover this floor? And what will I put in that funky little corner?
- How many bricks do I need to build these walls to the same height?
- This window frame isn't an even number of bricks tall. How will I install it and still make the walls even?
- How will I support the second floor and leave an opening for the stairs?
- How many shingles do I need to cover the roof?
- I want to add a balcony. How will I support it?
- There's no more of this part. How will I finish this project?

Suppose you've just built something, but you want to change it up. Maybe add a floor or change the windows. How many additional pieces will you need? If you're ordering online, how many pieces come in a package? How many packages will you need to complete your project? To answer these questions, you need to be able to visualize a space in three dimensions, and think in proportions, just like construction workers. It's also a fun way to practice geometry.

Just like a real construction project, your model needs to have balance and symmetry, or it won't fit together—or stay together.

TILE AND MARBLE SETTERS

Marble, granite, and tile are enduring materials. They were used to create ancient buildings and artwork. Many ancient Greek temples are still standing—at least partially—and can be visited. Ancient Roman tile mosaics still exist. The Taj Mahal was built out of marble as an Indian mausoleum in the 17th century and remains one of the wonders of the world.

Today, smooth, white marble and glittering granite are welcome touches of luxury. Homeowners choose colorful tiles for their kitchens and bathrooms—two rooms everyone spends time in every day. Tile and marble setters put hard tile, marble, and wooden tiles on all kinds of surfaces, including walls, floors, countertops, patios, and roof decks. They measure and cut the tiles or marble they need, then arrange them by following a design plan and instructions from architects, builders, or homeowners. The workers prepare and apply mortar or another adhesive. They then install tile and marble in the area and fill the spaces between the pieces with grout or mortar using a rubber trowel. Decorative work such as tile or marble is expected to be in higher demand in the future, especially in expensive homes. Because some of this work takes place outdoors, consistent work is more common in warmer climates. Although you don't need a formal certification to work as a tile setter, obtaining one is usually a ticket to higher pay.

After graduating high school, consider an apprenticeship through a building contractor or a union. The International Masonry Institute's National Training Center, located in Bowie, Maryland, offers a

A cement mixer is a large truck that both mixes cement and transports it to the site where it's needed.

National Terrazzo Training Program for apprentices. Terrazzo work is often decorative. It's a good option for someone who's detailed and creative.

Cement masons, or cement finishers, use concrete, one of the world's toughest materials, to form the bases for buildings, patios, floors, dams, and roads. Factories, office buildings, hotels, shopping malls, and schools always require good cement masons. Concrete masons place and finish the concrete. Although cement and concrete seem like basic materials, masons need a thorough understanding of how they react to weather conditions and changes in temperature. After all, these are often the materials that hold up the entire structure.

FREEMASONRY

Freemasonry is the oldest fraternal organization in the world. Its origins go back to the medieval stonemasons' guilds. Those were the men who built the great cathedrals that still stand today. Modern Freemasonry dates to the 17th century Age of Enlightenment, when educated men gathered to discuss new ideas. Although Freemasons are no longer master craftsmen, many are influential men who have shaped society. President George Washington and statesman Benjamin Franklin were masons. So was astronaut Buzz Aldrin.

Medieval stonemasons created soaring cathedrals that still stand. They built them without computers or cranes.

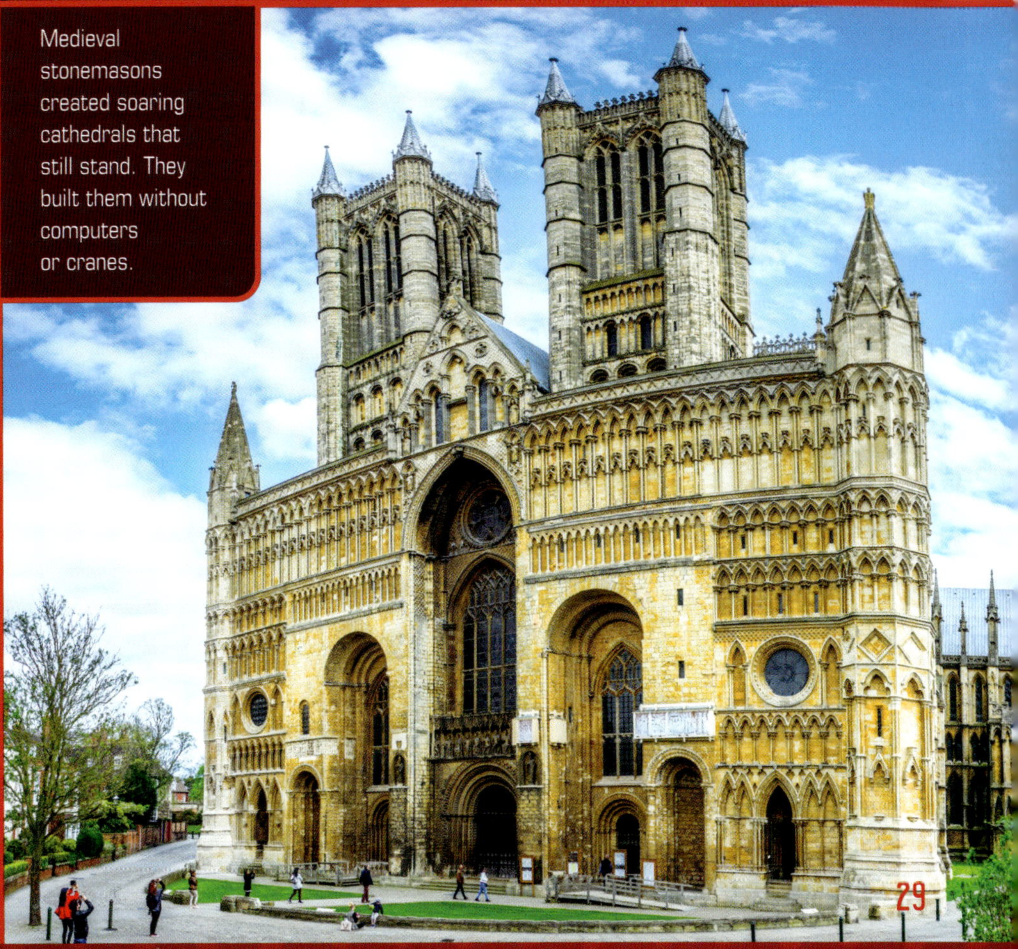

CHAPTER THREE

BUILDING WITH METAL

Heavy steel beams form the skeleton of many buildings. The steel frame of a new building is probably the iconic mental picture most people have of a construction site. But metal figures in other parts of the job. Pipes are metal. So are window and door frames, as well as doors. All that metal must be measured, cut, installed, and connected. It's hard, heavy work that can be dangerous. Construction professionals who work with metal must be safety conscious, detail oriented, and have nerves of—well, steel.

This steel frame will hold up an entire building.

WELDERS

When heat, pressure, or both are applied to the edges of two or more pieces of metal, they are permanently fused, or joined. This process is called welding. Welding creates and repairs products, from household appliances and pipes to vehicles and missiles. Construction workers who do it are called welders, solderers, and brazers. There are more than 80 different kinds of welding processes. Brazers connect copper pipes and other thinner metals with a filler metal that needs a higher temperature than used in typical welding. Brazing sometimes creates a protective coating against wear and tear. Welding is dangerous work. Welders need to have intense concentration. They always need to wear full PPE when working and be aware of their surroundings. They must always know and follow safety rules.

Girls and women can train to be welders, too. Attention to details and the ability to follow strict safety protocols are some of the most important traits for this field.

Some high schools offer courses in welding. A very few (five schools in the United States as of 2022) are accredited American Welding Society (AWS) testing facilities where students can earn their certification. Students who don't have access to one of those programs should consider blueprint reading, math, physics, chemistry, and mechanical drawing. Entry-level welders can learn on the job over a couple of weeks or up to three years for more skilled welding. Apprentice programs are offered through trade unions such as the International Association of Machinists and Aerospace Workers. With additional training and experience, welders can become supervisors, sales representatives, or welding inspectors. Welding engineers usually have a bachelor's degree. The AWS offers certification

This welder is wearing PPE to protect themselves from the heat and sparks generated by their work.

programs that are required for certain positions. Some programs offer computer classes that are necessary to learn how to run machines or even robots.

IRON AND STEEL WORKERS

Often called ironworkers or erectors, structural iron and steel workers build bridges, buildings, and frames for tall buildings and skyscrapers by putting in steel or iron beams. They also gather the cranes and loading cranes known as derricks that help move heavy tools and materials, such as huge lengths of steel and iron and buckets of concrete, around the construction site. They might also assemble metal buildings. Ironworkers follow blueprints or other instructions provided by construction supervisors to connect all the steel columns and beams together. Ironworkers also cut, bend, and weld steel using metal shears, torches, and other welding tools. Reinforcing iron and rebar workers insert metal rods or mesh into concrete forms. This makes the concrete stronger.

Iron workers should be comfortable working at great heights while only standing on narrow beams. Iron beams are heavy, and workers must be able to guide them into place and tighten bolts. At the same time, workers are on their feet for hours at a time. Most iron workers begin as apprentices through unions and contractor associations. An apprenticeship lasts three to four years and combines technical instruction with paid, on-the-job training. Some learn on the job. Certification in welding is considered a bonus by employers, as is serving in the military.

BOILERMAKERS

Boilers heat water or other liquid solutions under high pressure to make electric power. This provides heat and power to buildings, ships, or factories. Boilermakers install, maintain, test, and repair building and construction boilers. They also work with vats and other containers that hold liquids and gases as well as huge pipes for dams. Some boilers are constructed of metal plates that are so big and heavy, a large crane must be used to lift them into place. In those cases, boilermakers direct the crane operator to place the pieces. Boilers may be made of steel, iron, copper, or stainless steel.

BUILDING YOUR DREAM HOME

There are many steps involved in building a house and many professionals involved in the process. According to the U.S. Census Bureau, building a new home takes about seven months and costs about $400,000.

New construction starts by leveling and preparing the site. This involves heavy machinery operators—people who use backhoes and bulldozers. Then, concrete workers pour the foundation.

Carpenters build framing, walls, floors, and the roof. So are stairs, interior walls, cabinets, and countertops.

Plumbers install the pipes that will connect your new house to the sewer and water lines. They'll also install sinks, showers, toilets, a water heater, and connections for garden hoses. One of the advantages of building a new home is being able to install high-efficiency plumbing fixtures that use less water.

Electricians will install wiring and HVAC professionals will install ductwork, a furnace or central air conditioning unit (possibly both), and thermostats. A benefit of new construction is that you can install smart appliances and systems designed to conserve energy. You might also choose to use solar power.

Painters or decorators will finish the inside walls with paint, wallpaper, and decorative trims. Flooring specialists will install hardwood, tile, or carpeting.

Finally, masons will install outside steps, a patio, and a driveway. Landscapers will make the outside look as attractive as the inside. You can choose eco-friendly plants and install a gray water irrigation system.

A big benefit of building a new home is that you can take advantage of all the latest water- and energy-conserving appliances and building techniques.

Boilermakers repair and construct the boilers with hand and power tools such as flame cutting torches, power saws, and welding equipment. Some boilermakers start out as pipe fitters or steamfitters since they require similar skills. They follow blueprints to confirm a building's pipe system. Many boilermakers are skilled welders.

Boilermaker work is dangerous, so workers must know every safety rule and wear protective gear. Sometimes boilermakers must work inside the boiler or vat to install or repair it. Other times they may need to be up on top. They need to be comfortable with either situation.

Boilermakers often work on contract—that is, they do one job at a time, instead of working for a company full time. Some work might take the boilermaker far from home for long stretches of time. They might also have downtime between contracts.

During high school, consider taking classes in math, welding, and blueprint reading. Most boilermakers take a four- to five-year apprenticeship program, but it takes less time if they have previous welding and work experience. Unions and contractor associations such as the International Brotherhood of Boilermakers offer training.

PLUMBERS

Plumbing is one construction trade that pretty much guarantees steady employment. However tight the economy is, people need access to fresh water, and sewage definitely needs to go where it's supposed to. People will call a plumber to do repair work, no matter what else they need to scrimp on.

Plumbers are called in whenever a house is being built and wherever there is water. They work wherever there are pipes and septic systems. They install pipes and fixtures and connect new buildings to municipal water and sewer systems.

Pipe fitters install and maintain pipes that carry chemicals, gases, and acids. Steamfitters install, repair, and maintain pipes that move steam under high pressure. Some plumbers specialize as gas fitters, who install oxygen pipes for hospital patients, and sprinkler fitters, who handle fire sprinkler systems.

Plumbing work can be tough. Materials might be as heavy as a cast iron bathtub weighing 350 pounds (159 kg). Plumbers climb ladders and work in small spaces. They might need to squeeze under a sink or open sheetrock to access pipes. They might need to work on pipes in basements where mold can be a factor. Some travel to multiple work sites each day. Because most of the work occurs

Plumbers often have to work in basements or crawlspaces. Dust, mold spores, and old insulation can be present in such places. Safety glasses and a respirator mask are appropriate PPE for these conditions.

indoors, plumbers can have employment all year round, no matter the weather.

During high school, students interested in plumbing should consider taking math, shop, chemistry, and physics classes. Some plumbers participate in an apprenticeship, or an on-the-job training program with an experienced plumber. Many states require a plumber to be licensed to work unsupervised. Technical school is another option. Plumbers need to read blueprints, learn safety, and know local codes and rules.

These are just some of the jobs available working with metal. For example, fabrication sheet metal workers make all sorts of precision parts. Installation sheet metal workers install things such as HVAC ducts, gutters, and siding. Maintenance sheet metal workers clean and repair ventilation systems. This makes them work more efficiently. Testing and balancing specialists adjust HVAC ducts to ensure the correct airflow to keep buildings comfortable. Sheet metal workers need to know how to read blueprints and technical diagrams. They're often trained welders.

UNIONS

A union is an organization of people who do the same sort of work. Unions use a technique called collective bargaining. This means that instead of a single person trying to negotiate a raise or correct a safety deficit, the union argues on behalf of all its members. If the union and the employer can't come to a settlement, workers go on strike. This can delay projects and cost the employer lots of money.

Unions negotiate fair pay, benefits, and safe working conditions for their members. Generally, union members make more money than nonunion workers. Workers pay dues to belong to the union. Part of that money often goes into a fund to pay workers if they go on strike. There are many unions that construction workers can join. These are just a few:

- North America's Building Trades Unions (NABTU)
- The United Association of Journeymen and Apprentices of the Plumbing and Pipefitting Industry of the United States and Canada (UA)
- The United Brotherhood of Carpenters and Joiners of America (UBC)
- The International Alliance of Theatrical Stage Employees, Moving Picture Technicians, Artists and Allied Crafts of the United States, Its Territories and Canada (IATSE) (This is a union for construction workers in the entertainment industry.)

Unions have argued for—and won—uniform workdays and workweeks, paid holidays, breaks, and many other things people tend to take for granted.

CHAPTER FOUR

OPERATING THE BIG MACHINES

Something you see at almost every construction site is a variety of big trucks and heavy machinery. Dump trucks, cranes, and backhoes are familiar sights. So are steamrollers and cement mixers.

Working with these machines can be dirty, greasy, muddy work. Much of the work is full time, but occasionally the hours can be irregular, overnight, and far from home. Large machine operators work in every climate and weather, although rain and cold can stop work sometimes. Most large machine operators maintain, repair, and clean their machines.

Workers who know how to operate multiple kinds of machines have the greatest advantage and can use their skills in other industries. Some workers might be eligible for the U.S. Department of Labor's Job Corps training and certification in heavy equipment operations. Courses generally take eight to twelve months to complete. Some operators train at vocational schools. Many train on the job, starting with lighter equipment and working their way up to more complex machines. Equipment operators tend to have a higher rate of injury and illness than other occupations, but safety guidelines and operating procedures help reduce accidents. Large machines such as bulldozers and pile drivers can shake and bump the driver up and down. These machines are also quite loud.

PILE DRIVER

Pile drivers operate a machine that forces piles into the ground. Driven piles are long, heavy beams of steel, concrete, or timber that support walls, building foundations, bridges, or other large structures. Sometimes piles are used to hold soil back from a construction site. Piles can be used underwater, and some pile drivers are also certified scuba divers, who are needed for working on underwater projects, such as building docks. Pile drivers also work on oil rigs.

COMMERCIAL DRIVER'S LICENSE

Construction vehicles are heavier and more complex than regular cars. Some machinery requires drivers to have a special license, a commercial driver's license (CDL), because particular skills are needed to operate them safely. Each state has its own rules and regulations. The first step to getting a CDL is to have a regular driver's license and a clean driving record. A CDL must be issued by the same state as your standard license. Once you hold a CDL, you must take particular care to keep your record clean. Serious traffic infractions—even while driving your personal vehicle on your own time—can impact your CDL.

According to the Federal Motor Carrier Safety Association, states must issue CDLs based on three classes of commercial motor vehicles (CMVs). Generally, classes A and B are based on the vehicle's weight, including anything it might be towing. Class C is based on the number of passengers it can carry or hazardous materials it could transport.

Some licenses need special endorsements, or additional requirements, such as to carry extra passengers or hazardous materials. Drivers must pass a test for each commercial endorsement.

ENDORSEMENT	VEHICLE TYPE	REQUIREMENTS
T	double/triple trailers	knowledge test
P	passenger vehicles	knowledge test and a skills test
N	tank vehicles	knowledge test
H	hazardous materials	knowledge test and the Transportation Security Administration test
X	tank vehicle/ hazardous materials combination	knowledge test and the Transportation Security Administration test

S	school bus	knowledge test and a skills test

Check your state's department of motor vehicles website for specific information about CDL rules and licenses, commercial driver handbooks, tests, and practice tests. Some commercial endorsements may also require a criminal background check.

A "pile driver" can mean the machine that hammers the piles into the ground or the person operating the machine. The machine may be mounted on skids, barges, or cranes. The job is physical and requires a lot of heavy lifting. Generally, operators move hand and foot levers to put pilings into place. They also push pedals and turn valves to start power hammers and to raise and lower the drop hammers that pound the piles into place. The job requires precision and safety is a constant concern. Pile drivers work outdoors in all sorts of weather.

Operating heavy construction equipment requires special training and possibly a permit or license.

During high school, math courses—especially geometry—will be a big help. So will any sort of shop classes offered in your school. Most pile drivers train through a union apprenticeship program. This means they're paid while they train and start their career with little to no student debt. In some states, pile driver operators may need a special crane operator certification or license. Certain states classify pile drivers as cranes, and 18 states require pile driver operators to have a crane license.

OPERATING ENGINEERS

When it comes time to excavate, transport, and grade dirt and rocks, operating engineers are on the job. They complete some of the heaviest work on a construction site. They pour concrete and other hard pavement as well as help erect structures. Operating engineers run power construction equipment such as front-end loaders, bulldozers, and tractors, to name a few. Sometimes they operate industrial trucks and tractors that lift material with forklifts and booms. They may also control power equipment such as air compressors and pumps that are on the construction site. All of this takes focus and concentration.

Safety is always on the mind of operating engineers. In fact, most construction workers are required to complete a special class from the Occupational Safety and Health Administration (OSHA). Because they operate such large heavy machines, they must always be aware of their surroundings. Before digging, operational engineers consult municipal maps and talk to utility companies.

They must know where wires or pipes might be buried underground so that they don't accidentally cut or burst them.

During high school, helpful classes might include automotive mechanics, mechanical drawing, science, and computers. Most jobs in this field require some training, such as vocational school, on-the-job-experience working with large machines, or an associate's degree. Sometimes completing a licensing exam is required. Some apprenticeships are available. With time and experience, construction equipment operators can advance to positions such as supervisor and trainer, or even open their own contracting businesses.

CRANE OPERATORS

Cranes are one of the most easily identifiable pieces of construction equipment. They're often the tallest vehicle on the site. There are overhead cranes, mobile cranes, and tower cranes. Some cranes are mounted on a truck, some move on their own, and others stay on a site where they are mounted on a tall structure.

It's important to wear the correct personal protective equipment (PPE) on a construction site. Besides a hardhat and steel-toed boots, safety glasses, noise canceling earmuffs, and respirators are all essential to keep workers safe.

If you live to party, a career in construction might not be for you. Construction workers need to have a clear head on the job. In addition, serious traffic infractions or a criminal record can cause your CDL to be revoked.

The crane has an area for the operator to sit, although some operators run the crane from a remote-control center on the site. Many controls are computerized. Crane and tower operators direct the mechanical boom, or tower, and cable to lift and move enormous and heavy machines and materials. They might dig out and lift dirt or even knock down walls with a wrecking ball. Using moving equipment, they move loads and containers to and from trucks. Crane and tower operators also work at ports, loading and unloading cargo ships. They might also work at steel mills. Other workers often help direct the operators by communicating with a radio or hand signals.

During high school, consider taking classes such as shop, auto mechanics, electronics, and science. Math such as algebra and calculus and mechanical drawing will help, too. Crane operators often start out as construction laborers and learn how to operate equipment. Others learn during an apprenticeship through the Associated General Contractors of America and the International Union of Operating Engineers. Many municipalities require a crane operator to have a special license or certification. To become certified in New York, a crane operator must show proof of training and pass a test. They also need to have good eyesight and hearing, and no heath conditions that could affect their job performance, such as epilepsy or a heart condition. The International Union of Operating Engineers is one place to attain a crane operating license for overhead, mobile, or tower cranes.

This section has covered just a sample of large machine operator jobs. In demolition work, large machines are used to take down buildings that can't be repaired. This is done very carefully to ensure that no nearby buildings are damaged and a minimum of debris is released into the air. Industrial truck and tractor operators drive trucks and tractors around worksites and warehouses. Excavating and loading machine and dragline operators use machines with shovels to move material such as sand and earth. Dredge operators excavate waterways. The road crew works on highways, airport runways and taxiways, and parking lots. From forklifts to cranes, there are all sorts of construction jobs involving heavy machinery and vehicles.

BIG MACHINES!

If we're honest with ourselves, most of us never quite outgrow our childhood fascination with all the big trucks and other huge construction vehicles. But what exactly do they do? And what qualifications do you need to operate them?

CONCRETE MIXER	mixes concrete and delivers it to the worksite	requires a commercial driver's license (CDL) to operate
FORKLIFT	used for lifting and moving things on pallets	requires professional certification
DUMP TRUCK	used to move loose material like dirt around a construction site	larger models require a CDL to operate
CRANE	used to lift large, heavy objects to great heights	requires a crane operator's license
BACKHOE	can be used to dig or push objects	larger models require a heavy equipment operator's license
ASPHALT PAVER	lays asphalt on a roadway	generally requires a CDL

A concrete mixer uses a chute to pour concrete exactly where it's needed on the construction site.

CHAPTER FIVE

HOW DO YOU BUILD A HOUSE?

Although construction workers build many things, homes are one of the most interesting—and most meaningful. Housing is a basic need. Building a home involves many kinds of construction professionals. They combine their skills to build a house that's comfortable, attractive, safe, and energy and water efficient. Any house—from a bungalow to a mansion-goes through many of the same steps.

CARPENTERS

Carpenters build with wood. Although that's one of the oldest methods of construction, carpenters need to be up on all the latest building technologies, including green, or sustainable construction. Carpenters generally build and repair a building's framework and structures, such as stairways and doorframes. Others build braces and scaffolding for buildings. This is called rough carpentry. Some carpenters also install cabinets, siding, floors, and drywall. This is called finish carpentry.

Carpenters work on everything from houses and buildings to bridges and highways. In addition to the framework for buildings, they also build the forms used to pour concrete. They follow blueprints and plans to cut and measure wood, plastic, and other materials. Carpenters work both inside and outside, depending on the type of construction job. They may work in tight spaces with a lot of lifting, standing, and kneeling.

The organization Habitat for Humanity has a youth program that accepts volunteers as young as age 5. During high school, classes to consider include carpentry and woodworking, math, science, and mechanical drawing. Most carpenters start out as apprentices, but others learn on the job. Apprentices learn basic carpentry, how to read blueprints, building codes, math, sketching, and safety and first aid. They're paid and receive benefits during their apprenticeship.

Two-year technical schools sometimes offer carpentry degrees in cooperation with unions or contractor organizations. Because carpenters learn so much about every angle of the construction business, they could become supervisors, foremen, or independent contractors.

A rough carpenter built the frame of this house. A finish carpenter is installing decorative trim.

ELECTRICIANS

Electricians are essential members of the construction crew. They install, maintain, and repair home, business, and factory heating, lighting, refrigeration, air-conditioning, and communications equipment. Electricians follow blueprints to figure out where to install heating, lighting, and cooling systems, as well as outlets, light fixtures, and switches. They also connect the new building to the municipal power grid.

Electricians may work inside or outside in almost every structure imaginable. Sometimes they must bend, lift, and kneel in small spaces. Injury such as shocks and burns are common. Even electrocution is possible. For these reasons, it's a good idea to be certified in first aid and cardiopulmonary resuscitation (CPR).

During high school, taking classes in science, shop, and math will be helpful. If owning your own business is appealing, consider contracting and management courses. Many electricians start out in technical school. Some start out as helpers to experienced electricians. Organizations such as the Independent Electrical Contractors (IEC) group and the International Brotherhood of Electrical Workers (IBEW) sponsor programs for apprentices. Most states require electricians to have a license. Sometimes electricians are required to take continuing education courses even after they have a license. These courses help them stay on top of new technologies and updates to the National Electrical Code, as well as building codes for the location where they work.

Electricians are involved throughout the construction process, from installing wiring and appliances to connecting the new house to the municipal power grid.

INSULATION CONTRACTORS

Insulation is material that's added inside the walls and roof of a house. It helps keep the house warm in winter and cool in summer. A well-insulated structure requires less energy to heat or cool. This helps lower utility bills.

Systems such as boilers, pipes, and refrigerated units need insulation, too. Floor, ceiling, and wall insulators put in insulation in attics and floors and behind walls. Mechanical insulators install insulation around pipes and ductwork in buildings such as factories and businesses. They also install thermal ignition barriers as required by local building codes.

The most common types of insulation are

fiberglass batts or spray foam. Insulation specialists measure and cut the insulation to the size and shape needed and apply it by spraying, stapling, taping, cementing, and even attaching with wire bands. Some insulation is covered with a material such as sheet metal to give it extra protection from the weather. When walls are insulated, workers put up wire mesh and the sprayed insulation sticks to it. Then a wall of plaster or panels can be put up over the insulation.

Insulation removal is a big part of the job, too. Unfortunately, this comes with some dangers if the building was constructed before 1974. Asbestos was once widely used for insulation, but the material was later found to cause cancer. Only workers who have been specially trained can remove asbestos from insulation. They are hazardous materials (hazmat) removal workers. They wear special suits and respirators while performing asbestos abatement. Special care must be taken to contain debris. New insulation can be installed only after all asbestos has been eliminated. Often this is a condition of selling a property or performing renovations.

HVAC TECHNICIANS

Walls and insulation aren't enough to keep a building comfortable. In most climates, people need to heat their homes in winter and cool them in summer—usually both. HVAC installers and mechanics put in, repair, and perform maintenance on air-conditioning and heaters. Most HVAC specialists work in homes, hospitals, schools, and businesses. They need to be familiar with all the latest energy-efficient and eco-friendly technologies. Although they might be trained to work on many different kinds, some specialize in one specific type of machine, such as furnaces or air conditioners. Others may focus on installation or repair.

Refrigeration (HVACR) workers take care of machines that make ice and keep food cold or frozen in hotels, restaurants, grocery stores, and homes. In facilities that serve food to the public, their services are critical. Health regulations state that food must be stored within a certain temperature range. Otherwise, it must be discarded. This costs money in lost meal revenue, upset customers, and replacement inventory.

Most HVAC and HVACR workers travel to different sites to work. They read blueprints and other design requirements to work on the heating and cooling. Most heating and cooling work is indoors, but some systems might be outdoors. Workers may have to work in small, uncomfortable spaces. If they are hired for repairs, it may be very hot or freezing cold.

During high school, consider classes in algebra, mechanical drawing, physics, and machine shop. Today, most HVAC and HVACR technicians have a certificate from a trade school or an associate's degree. North American Technician Excellence (NATE) is one source for HVAC and HVACR certification. Many states require HVAC and HVACR workers to pass a test and have a license. In addition, the Environmental Protection Agency (EPA) requires workers who handle refrigerants to be certified in the safe handling of those chemicals.

ROOFERS

A good roof is vitally important to the value and comfort of a building. A well-insulated roof helps keep in heating and air conditioning and keep out weather. Roofers cover the tops of buildings with materials including tar, shingles, tiles, slate, rubber, wood, and even asphalt. Sometimes they spray materials to bind, insulate, or waterproof the top of a building. They also work on swimming pools, walls, and other building surfaces to protect them from dampness and water. Roofing work involves repair or replacement, so even when the construction industry is not hopping, roofers have plenty of work. Even a small leak can cause devastating damage to a structure.

Most buildings have composition roofing such as built-up roofing, which is made up of layers of hot asphalt or felt covered with tar. Sometimes workers nail or cement asphalt shingles or rolls of roofing material to the roof. Single-ply roofing seals seams with special cements, hot-air welders, and solvent welding using butane or propane torches. Roofers must take special courses to become certified to

Roofers need to be extremely conscious of personal safety. According to the BLS, roofing contractors were involved in 123 fatal accidents in 2021. Ninety-nine of them were falls.

use these materials. Rows of tile and slate shingles overlap on top of felt over a wood base. Finally, roofers or sheet metal workers can install metal roofing. Some metal roofs are made up of cookie pan–sized sheets of metal soldered together. Standing seam roofing has seams that stick up where sheets of metal are connected.

There are no specific licensing requirements for roofers, other than standard OSHA training. The National Roofing Contractors Association offers certification in some roofing specialties.

Roofers get tired, hot, and dirty. They should have good balance and be confident at heights. Math skills are important, as well as the ability to communicate clearly and follow directions. Although most building jobs are scheduled for the spring and summer, roofers can be called upon to make emergency repairs at any time of the year. However, severe weather may keep them from work if conditions are unsafe.

During high school, students can gain experience by getting a part-time or summer job as a roofer's helper. Many begin as trainees or apprentices, working with more experienced roofers.

PAINTERS AND DECORATORS

Once the walls and ceilings are up, it's time to make them look nice and protect that hard work. Paint, stain, enamel, and varnish might seem like they're applied for decoration, but they actually protect the surfaces, especially outdoors, where weather can wear them out. Painters don't just choose pretty colors. They must select the right kind of paint for the surface they're working on, such as wood, plaster, or concrete. Painters may also work on walls, buildings, bridges, and equipment. They apply substances using brushes, rollers, and spray machines. Sometimes they must remove old paint by scraping, or the surface might need to be cleaned. They must spackle or fill holes or cracks to make sure the surface is smooth. Painters mix colors and oils to achieve a certain color or texture. They might also apply primer before they paint or sealant after to preserve the paint job.

Painters work inside and outdoors. Residential painters paint the interiors and exteriors of houses. They may work while a family is in residence, as well as on new construction. Commercial painters work on offices and other nonresidential buildings and structures. Painters working on bridges should be comfortable with heights. They may have to work in uncomfortable positions, sometimes suspended from ropes or cables. Some painters put up scaffolds, too. Injury and illness among painters are very common. They may fall, strain muscles, or experience irritation from plaster dust.

Although painters and decorators are some of the last construction professionals to work on a project, their work is often the most visible.

Most painters learn their craft on the job, but some learn through an apprenticeship. Anyone interested in industrial painting can earn a certification through the National Association of Corrosion Engineers. Painters need to have a thorough understanding of the chemicals they use, and the need for adequate ventilation.

Many painters and decorators are employed by a contractor to work on new buildings, remodeling, and restoration. They need to have a good eye for color and be up to date on the latest trends. Painters also work in the maintenance departments of schools, apartment complexes, or hospitals, to name just a few. With experience, a painter can become a supervisor, a job estimator, or a superintendent (who takes care of a building).

GLAZIERS

Glaziers install and repair glass in storefronts, skylights, mirrors, or even tabletops. A glazier chooses the best glass for a project. For example, glass for store windows is often tinted or coated so that merchandise on display doesn't become faded from the sun. Then the glass is cut, fit to the space, and installed. The glazier might file or smooth edges, too.

Construction companies, glass companies, and glazing contractors all employ glaziers. Factories where glass items such as windows are put together also hire glaziers. Work might be indoors or outdoors at a site. Some glaziers drive the truck to deliver materials and supplies to the job site.

Glaziers stand, bend, and stretch all day long. They lift large, heavy pieces of glass and other awkward objects and move them into place. Some work at great heights. This line of work is one of the more dangerous, with chances of cuts from glass and sharp tools. Glaziers might also be exposed to solvents.

During high school, math classes will be the most useful. Most glaziers start out as helpers on the job with local contractors or unions, but they must complete a training program or a three-year apprenticeship. Some states require glaziers to be licensed.

This is just an overview of some of the major jobs that help build a house. Drywall installers measure and put in sheetrock (layers of plaster sandwiched between two sheets of thick paper) for walls and ceilings.

Floor installers put down blocks, strips, or sheets of floor coverings. These coverings usually make the floors easier to stand and walk on (shock absorbing), keep them from making too much noise, and make them look nice. Carpet installers are responsible for plush floor coverings in all kinds of buildings. Floor coverings not only need to look good, but they also need to be appropriate for the location. For instance, a pale-colored carpet won't last in a high traffic public corridor. There are certifications available for professional floor coverers.

Larger buildings, such as apartment complexes and factories, need elevators installed. They will also need sprinkler systems and fire alarms. Specialists will install telephone, internet, and security systems.

REALITY TV

Like almost every other topic these days, there are reality TV shows about the construction industry. Some have to do with actual building projects, such as *This Old House*. Others, including *Flip or Flop*, concern home makeovers. *Building Off the Grid* showcases sustainable building practices.

There are also shows such as *Modern Marvels* or *Impossible Engineering*. These focus on some of the most incredible engineering feats in the world.

While we all know that reality TV isn't always an accurate reflection of, well, reality, these shows can give you ideas about what sort of career you'd like to pursue.

You don't need to confine your dreams to building houses. Construction workers design and build bridges and skyscrapers, too.

CHAPTER SIX

WHO MAKES THE BIG DECISIONS?

Planners, leaders, and managers have more experience on the job and more training than entry-level workers. They may have advanced through the ranks of apprenticeship to become journey workers, then foremen, then supervisors. Or they might hold multiple college degrees. It depends on the type of work they do. These positions come with more responsibilities, higher stress, and sometimes longer hours, but they're often compensated with higher salaries.

ARCHITECTS

Architects help plan and design places where people live, work, and play. They work together with clients to bring their vision to life. In general, architects focus on buildings and other structures, from a small entryway to an entire college campus. They must consider the safety of everyone who will be in and around the building.

Landscape architects design beautiful yet useful land areas, such as gardens, playgrounds, or highways. They plan locations for buildings, roadways, and walkways, as well as where to plant trees and flowers. Sometimes landscape architects help design areas that need to be restored, such as wetlands. This is called environmental remediation. Architects mostly work in offices, but they do visit job sites to check on work progress. Many architects work more than 50 hours each week, according to the U.S. Bureau of Labor Statistics. Some work from home offices.

During high school, helpful classes include mechanical drawing, art, history, physics, and math. Some students can find part-time jobs or internships in architectural firms. Many students study to earn a professional degree from a program approved by the National Architectural Accrediting Board (NAAB). All students must take part in the Intern Development Program (IDP), pass the Architect Registration Exam (ARE), and get a license. Many architects go on to earn a master's degree.

Sometimes architects build models of their designs. This can help a client visualize what the project will look like.

DRAFTERS

Once the engineer or architect has a design ready, the drafter steps in. Drafters use computer-aided design (CAD) software to make drawings and convert them into technical designs and plans used in construction and production. For this reason, they may also be referred to as CAD operators. Their drawings must show exact measurements, materials, and instructions.

Drafters work at computers most of the time. They usually work full time, and overtime is fairly common. Most drafters work for engineering and drafting services companies and architectural and landscape businesses.

During high school, consider taking classes such as mathematics, science, computer technology, design, computer graphics, and drafting. Drafters generally hold an associate of applied sciences degree or a certificate from a trade school. These programs take about two years to complete. The American Design Drafting Association (ADDA) offers drafting certification programs. With experience, a drafter might be able to advance to become a supervisor.

Even though a great deal of design work is done on computers today, it's still good to have manual drawing skills.

ALL ABOUT ENGINEERING

There are many kinds of engineers that work on construction projects. Civil engineers plan and supervise construction projects. They're assisted by civil engineering technicians. Civil engineering is a broad field that includes several specialties.

Structural engineers plan and evaluate large-scale projects such as tunnels and dams to make sure they're safe and secure. Structural engineers get to spend a lot of time outdoors on worksites. Construction engineers supervise building projects. They may also be responsible for any temporary buildings used on the site during the project.

Geotechnical engineers make sure the foundations on which structures will be built are solid. They study how the earth—soil, water, and rocks—will withstand the buildings and bridges built on it by engineers. They also make plans for tunnels and retaining walls, which hold back soil or water.

Transportation engineers create transportation systems such as highways, airways, and railroad systems. They draw and review plans for transportation projects and check calculations.

Aside from civil engineers, there are also mechanical engineers. Some mechanical engineers work as heating and cooling system engineers. They design environmental systems for use in places like schools or computer rooms. There are also electrical engineers who design electrical equipment, including systems that generate power. They might be involved in constructing power plants or factories.

CIVIL ENGINEERS

Civil engineers research, plan, design, and supervise large-scale construction jobs such as power plants and roads. This is precision work, as thousands of people utilize infrastructure. Civil engineers work in the office but check on job progress at the construction site. Researchers may work in a laboratory.

In high school, courses such as math, science, English, social studies, and computers are useful. So are classes related to communications and public speaking, as civil engineers oversee other construction professionals. Internships may be available at engineering firms, local planning offices, and construction companies. The National Association of Colleges and Employers (NACE) website is a good place to start looking.

Civil engineering technicians assist civil engineers. They need to earn an associate's degree. Civil engineers generally need a bachelor's degree. Licensing requirements vary my location. Generally, if a civil engineer wants to advance, they need to be licensed as a professional engineer and pursue a graduate degree. Professional engineers must attend a school accredited by Accreditation Board for Engineering and Technology (ABET) and pass the Fundamentals of Engineering exam.

CONTRACTORS

Contractors—also called construction managers, general contractors, project managers, foremen, or project engineers—oversee a construction project from (just about) beginning to end and keep it on schedule. They often bid on jobs and must figure out what tools, equipment, and materials to use. Clients want their project completed for as little money as possible. A contractor's bid must include materials that are up to code and properly licensed professionals to carry out the work. It can be a fine line to tread.

Some contractors work on many kinds of projects, but most specialize in residential, commercial, or industrial structures. Each kind of project has different standards and requires different tools and equipment. On large projects, several foremen may be hired to work on different parts of it. Because contractors work on many stages of a project, they're responsible for hiring workers to do each part, such as electricians, carpenters, and masons. Independent contractor Larry Cavagnaro says, "I meet and work with a lot of interesting people, and I get to work on really great sites with nice houses. Each day is different."

For homeowners, the benefit of hiring a contractor is that they're responsible for getting the whole job done. They hire masons, carpenters or whatever other kind of professional is required. They get the materials, arrange delivery, and clean up afterwards.

COST ESTIMATORS

Every project has a budget. Whether it's a homeowner renovating their bathroom or a town building a new high school, there's a set amount of money available for the project. Therefore, every construction job needs an estimate of how much time, money, materials, and labor will be needed. Cost estimators answer those questions to help clients decide whether to build a structure or renovate an existing one. They also figure out whether a job is making money. Most cost estimators work in the construction industry, but some work in manufacturing or other services.

Cost estimators need to make accurate estimates because several other contractors may be bidding for the same job. Usually, the company that makes the lowest bid gets the job to do the work. Cost estimators need to consider every aspect of the work. Ron Moore, general manager of Western Building Restoration Company, also does cost estimates. An estimator has "to figure the cost of the job high enough to make a profit, but low enough to be awarded the project," he says. If an estimator's bid is too high, the company may not get the job. If it's too low, the company risks losing money when the project is done. They need to consider local laws and building codes. Materials must meet fire standards, and certain kinds of work—often plumbing and electrical—need to be performed by licensed professionals, not basic day laborers.

Cost estimators mostly work at the office in front of a computer, but they often travel to the worksite. They work under a lot of stress to meet deadlines with good estimates. They can't cut corners to lower the price because the structure might not pass inspection. Worse, there could be an accident that hurts people.

During high school, consider classes in math and accounting, as well as reading plans, blueprints, mechanical drawing, computers, and drafting. Most cost estimators have a college degree in building construction, building science, construction management, architecture, or engineering. They'll receive additional on the job training in CAD and other specialty software. If they don't have a college degree, Moore suggests "hands-on experience in the trades of the field."

Cost estimators need to figure in every aspect of a project—labor, materials, permits, and insurance.

CONSTRUCTION AND BUILDING INSPECTORS

Construction and building inspectors make sure that all construction work follows local and national regulations. All repairs, changes, and new construction on buildings, bridges, homes, and highways, as well as electrical work, elevators, and plumbing, must be legal and safe. Municipalities have rules about new construction. Some address obvious safety concerns, such as unsafe steps or wiring. Other rules concern things such as how close a building can come to the property line or obstructing a scenic view. Wendell Cook, a self-employed home inspector, says, "I inspect homes looking for defects [and] items in need of repair or replacement, and describe needed maintenance." Usually, inspections occur at the beginning of construction with follow-up inspections as progress is made and a final inspection when the work is completed.

A surveyor determines the exact boundaries of a piece of property before any building begins.

Most of a building inspector's time is spent outdoors at job sites, but they also spend time in the office reviewing plans and blueprints and scheduling appointments. A city building inspector reviews applications for permits, issues them, and inspects the work when it's complete. They might also respond to complaints, such as a tenant complaining about rats or other unsafe conditions in an apartment building. They may have to climb ladders or wriggle through small, cramped spaces.

Home inspectors are often hired when a house is for sale. The current owner might want an assessment before putting the house on the market. A prospective buyer might want an expert opinion before making an offer.

During high school, classes such as drafting, algebra, geometry, shop, and English are helpful. Inspectors usually need a lot of experience in the construction industry, which can be learned on the job. Some learn building codes and standards on their own or work with experienced inspectors. Cook suggests, "Learn everything you can about how a home works, [and] if possible, find a mentor who will train and teach you."

Many employers prefer an apprenticeship or an associate's or bachelor's degree that includes courses in building inspection, home inspection, construction technology, and drafting. Many states require inspectors to be licensed or certified by associations such as the International Code Council or the International Association of Electrical Inspectors. Some municipalities also require inspectors to complete regular continuing education.

When a new building is constructed, its impact on the environment and infrastructure is carefully reviewed.

Plenty of other upper-level jobs are available in construction. For example, before the first bulldozer hits the soil, the land must be studied. It must be mapped and measured to show precisely what it looks like and what, if anything, should be changed for construction to start. The exact position of a building must be marked. The construction surveyor works with civil engineers, landscape architects, and other planners to map out the property and locate the boundaries. Surveyor's generally need a bachelor's degree and license.

For some projects, an environmental specialist may be called in. They check the proposed building site to see what kinds of wildlife live there. They determine if the proposed project would impact wildlife or waterways.

GREEN CONSTRUCTION

Green construction is also called sustainable building. It's the process of building a structure that has minimal environmental impact. A green building might use recycled materials or wood from sustainable forests. Solar power is a popular green building option. So are features such as a gray water system that directs used water from sinks or washing machines to flush toilets or irrigate landscaping. Green buildings often use state-of-the-art insulation so they require less energy for heating and cooling. They might use low-flow toilets and showers, and energy-efficient appliances.

Green building techniques sometimes cost more to install but save money on energy and water in the long run.

CHAPTER SEVEN

FINDING YOUR FIRST JOB

Once you've decided on a career in construction. you must search and apply for a job. Once you land that job, it's important to know how to keep it. Your résumé and cover letter are two of the most important tools for your job search. A cover letter is a first impression, so it should be professional and well written. Although a résumé outlines education and work experience, a cover letter is an opportunity to expand on that. If you have a mutual acquaintance, or if you know someone who already works there, a cover letter is the perfect time to mention it.

The contents of your résumé will depend on your age and where you are in your training. If you're attending a technical school, there's probably an advisor who can help you. If you're a union apprentice, the union's website probably has a job board.

A résumé should be brief and to the point, so one page is usually enough. It's good to start out listing your work experience, beginning with your most recent work. The same goes for listing job responsibilities and specific qualifications or specialties. For samples of different styles of résumés,

there are plenty of examples online. The job website Monster.com even has sample résumés for all kinds of construction jobs.

Don't worry if you don't have specialized education or much experience. Any work experience demonstrates your work ethic and responsibility. Office or organizational skills and customer service are things you'll use in any job setting.

Make sure all information on your résumé is true and can be backed up. Most employers do a background check, including online searches. Having any kind of criminal record might not exclude you from consideration, but lying about it definitely will. Using professional language, proper grammar, and correct spelling shows you're serious about the job. Proofread any letters, notes, or résumés for spelling and grammar before they're sent out. Slowly and carefully read the text out loud. Have someone you trust listen to you read the letter out loud, and have

Your first contact with a potential employer might be via phone. "'Sup bro?" is not a good first impression.

him or her read it, too. Another person might see or hear mistakes.

Since most job applications are online, consider setting up a separate email address—one that doesn't use any rude words or strange abbreviations. Something simple like your name @ free email service works just fine. When communicating via email, spell out all the words and don't use emojis. Be sure to run a spell check. While you're waiting to hear back from a potential employer, be mindful of how you answer your phone, and be sure your voice mail message identifies you and doesn't contain any loud music, weird noise, or rude words.

THE INTERVIEW

Once you've gotten a call for an interview, research the company. Study the company's history, structure, and what it does. This helps decide how your skills will benefit it. Be sure to work this knowledge into the interview. It's important to make a good first impression, so be sure to look neat for the interview. If you're interviewing for an office position, a shirt and tie, possibly with a jacket, is appropriate. For many other jobs, khakis, and a collared shirt—office casual—works well. Just be sure everything you wear is neat, clean, and wrinkle free. If the interview is at a work site, be sure to wear appropriate footwear—just be sure your shoes are clean. Be sure your hair and nails are neat and clean and avoid heavy fragrances.

Have a few questions ready to ask during the meeting. Ask questions to get a sense of what it's like to work at the company, as well as what the other employees are like. In addition to helping you understand the company, asking questions shows that you're interested in them, too. Don't ask about money or benefits until you've been offered a job.

Even if you completed an application online, you may be asked to fill out another, so be sure to bring all your important papers to the interview. These can include copies of your résumé and cover letter, high school or college transcripts, or certificates that prove any certifications you might have. Before the interview, consider asking former managers or bosses to write letters of recommendation. These could discuss your hard work or other good qualities on the job. You'll probably be asked for your driver's license or other government-issued photo identification.

STARTING WORK

Congratulations! You applied for a job, got an interview, and were hired. That's a great accomplishment! However, you still need to prove yourself to keep the job. In most situations, new hires are on probation, usually for 90 days. This means you don't receive any paid time off or holiday pay. It also means managers are keeping an eye on you. They'll record patterns of tardiness or absenteeism. If management doesn't think you're a good fit for the company, you may be asked to leave.

- Check your schedule and know when you're supposed to be at work. Employers expect you to be at your station and ready to work at the start of your shift, not pulling into the parking lot.

- Construction work requires a clear head. Get a good night's sleep before work. Don't stay out partying.
- Know who you're supposed to call if you're sick and how much notice you're expected to give.
- Turn off your phone and pay attention to what you're supposed to be doing while on the job.
- Respect your coworkers. Even if you just graduated with a degree, they have real world experience.
- Do your job to the best of your ability. If you don't understand something, ask for help.
- Pay attention and take notes during your training and orientation. People don't mind answering questions for the new guy, but if you keep asking to have the basics explained over and over, they start to get annoyed.
- Wear the appropriate clothes and shoes for your work site. Always wear any required PPE.

The best thing you can bring to a new job is a good attitude and willingness to learn.

During the interview, use your best manners, speak clearly, and be polite. Sit up straight and make eye contact. Consider practicing a few lines to introduce yourself. Some people like to prepare an elevator pitch. Also known as a personal brand statement or a 30-second commercial, it's just a two- or three-sentence speech to have ready when someone asks you to tell him or her about yourself. It should combine your interests and strengths, some background, and why you are interested in working in the construction industry. This may also help you relax when you start the interview. It helps some people to practice not only their elevator pitch but also their interview skills. Have a friend or family member pretend to interview you so that you can practice introducing yourself, answering questions, and asking questions. A good interviewer wants you to be comfortable and make a good impression. At the conclusion of the interview, thank the interviewer for their time and shake hands.

Be courteous to anyone you encounter at the interview site. They might be your interviewer, the president of the company, or their biggest client.

Roofers, masons, carpenters, and other construction professionals will make this house safe again.

A FULFILLING CAREER CHOICE

The construction industry is a broad field that offers many opportunities. They range from jobs that can be started right after high school to careers that require graduate degrees. One of the most appealing aspects of the construction industry is the range of careers that begin as apprenticeships. Many construction professionals can begin their careers with little to no student debt.

Regardless of what's happening with the economy, there's almost always work for construction professionals. Even if there are no new projects, old buildings need to be renovated. And of course, there's always emergency repair work. As you gain experience, you can take additional classes to learn new specialties. In time, you might become a supervisor or manager. You might also decide to turn your talents to training the next generation of construction workers. Whether you want to work in an office or be outside all day, if you're not afraid of hard work (and heights!) there's a construction career for you.

Being part of a team that comes together to build large structures is very satisfying.

10 GREAT QUESTIONS TO ASK A CONSTRUCTION WORKER

Here are some questions you can ask a construction worker. Try to speak to professionals in different construction fields to get different perspectives.

1. Did you attend trade school, college, or complete an apprenticeship?
2. Why did you choose your field?
3. Are there any blogs or magazines you recommend?
4. Do you plan to continue your training and become a supervisor?
5. Do you work for a company or are you self-employed?
6. Do you prefer working on new buildings or doing renovations? Why?
7. What's your dream job?
8. Are there any classes or extracurricular activities I should be taking now?
9. Do you belong to a union or professional organization?
10. Is there anything you wish someone had told you when you started in this industry?

What other questions can you think of?

It's very exciting to build something that thousands of people will use for many years to come.

GLOSSARY

accredited: Given official authorization that standards have been met.

adhesive: A sticky substance used to join things together.

blueprint: A detailed plan, sometimes a print of a photograph, used to copy maps, technical drawings, or architectural plans.

boiler: A container that boils water to create steam.

boom: A long arm called a beam that extends upward at an angle to guide or support objects being moved.

certification: Proof that one has met special qualifications in a field of study.

drywall: A type of board made out of plaster, often used to build the inside walls of houses.

excavate: To create a hole by cutting, digging, or scooping, usually using a large machine.

facade: The face or front of a building, often facing the road or street.

grade: To level off or smooth a surface.

insulation: The material used to prevent the transfer of heat, cold, or noise. It is sometimes made up of acrylic, Styrofoam, and chemicals.

journeyperson or journey worker: A trained worker. The term journeyman is outdated and non-inclusive.

mausoleum: A large tomb, usually a grand stone building.

mortar: A combination of cement, sand, and water that keeps stones in place when it dries.

scaffolding: A temporary or movable framework or platform usually made of wood planks and metal poles that helps workers reach sites above ground level.

septic: Describing systems used to remove waste from a building.

solvent: Usually a liquid substance used to dissolve another substance.

stucco: A mixture of cement, lime, and sand.

subcontractor: A person or business that works for a company as part of a larger project.

union: An organized group of workers joined to protect their rights; sometimes called a labor union.

ventilate: To cause fresh air to move through an area.

vocational: Describing education or training aimed at skills for a specific occupation.

FOR MORE INFORMATION

AMERICAN COUNCIL FOR CONSTRUCTION EDUCATION (ACCE)

300 Decker Drive, Suite 330
Irving, Texas 75062
(972) 600-8800
Website: www.acce-hq.org
Facebook: @accehq.org
Instagram: @acceinsta
ACCE promotes, supports, and accredits quality construction educational programs.

AMERICAN DESIGN DRAFTING ASSOCIATION (ADDA)

230 East Main Street
2nd Floor
Newbern, TN 38059
(731) 627-0802
Website: www.adda.org
ADDA was established in 1948. It is the oldest professional organization for the graphics profession.

AMERICAN SOCIETY OF CIVIL ENGINEERS (ASCE)

1801 Alexander Bell Drive
Reston, VA 20191
(800) 548-2723
Website: www.asce.org
Facebook: @ASCE.org
Instagram: @asce_hq
The ASCE was founded in 1852. It's the oldest engineering society in the United States and represents 150,000 members.

ASSOCIATED BUILDERS AND CONTRACTORS

440 1st St., NW, Suite 200
Washington, D.C. 20001
(202) 595-1505
Website: abc.org
Facebook: @ABCNational
Instagram: @abc_national
ABC is a national construction industry trade association founded in 1950.

ASSOCIATED GENERAL CONTRACTORS OF AMERICA (AGC)

2300 Wilson Boulevard
Suite 300
Arlington, VA 22201
(703) 548-3118
Website: www.agc.org
Facebook: @AGCofA
AGC is a professional organization for general contractors.

CANADIAN CONSTRUCTION ASSOCIATION (CCA)

250 Albert Street, Suite 300
Ottawa, ON K1P 6M1
Canada
(613) 236-9455
Website: www.cca-acc.com
The CCA is the voice of the businesses, contractors, and suppliers involved in the Canadian commercial and industrial construction industry.

CANADIAN CONSTRUCTION WOMEN (CCW)

925 West Georgia Street
Suite 1200
Vancouver, BC V6C 3L2
Canada
Website: www.constructionwomen.org
Facebook: @cdnconstrcutionwomen
Instagram: @constrctionw
CCW is a professional development organization for women in the construction industry.

HOME BUILDERS INSTITUTE (HBI)

1201 15th Street NW, Sixth Floor
Washington, D.C. 20005
(202) 371-0600
Website: www.hbi.org
Facebook and Instagram: @HBIBuildingcareers
The HBI provides free pre-apprenticeship training in the trades.

JOB CORPS

200 Constitution Avenue NW, Room N4459
Washington, D.C. 20210
(800) 733-JOBS [5627]
Website: www.jobcorps.gov
Facebook, Instagram, and Twitter: @DOLJobCorps
The Job Corps is Department of Labor program that provides free job training for young people.

NATIONAL ASSOCIATION OF HOME BUILDERS

1201 Fifteenth St. NW
Washington, D.C. 20005
(800) 368-5242
Website: nahb.org
Facebook: @NAHBHome
Instagram: @homebuilders
The HBA works to improve workforce development in the construction trades.

NATIONAL FIRE PROTECTION ASSOCIATION

1 Batterymarch Park
Quincy, MA 02169-7471
(617) 770-3000
Website: nfpa.org
Facebook: @theNFPA
Instagram: @nfpadotorg
Twitter: @nfpa
The NFPA is a nonprofit agency dedicated to fire safety and prevention. They publish the National Electrical Code (NEC).

NATIONAL ASSOCIATION OF WOMEN IN CONSTRUCTION (NAWIC)

327 S. Adams Street
Fort Worth, TX 76104
(800) 552-3506
Website: www.nawic.org
Facebook and Instagram: @nawicnational
The NAWIC was offers education and networking opportunities to women in the construction industry.

FOR FURTHER READING

Astbury, Jon. *The Architecture Book*. New York, NY: DK, 2023.

Carosso, Juan. *At Your Best as an Electrician: Your Playbook for Building a Successful Career and Launching a Thriving Small Business as an Electrician (At Your Best Playbooks)*. New York, NY: Skyhorse Publishing, 2018.

Hughes, Karl, and Jennifer Wisdom. *Millennials' Guide to the Construction Trades: What No One Ever Told You About a Career in Construction*. Winding Pathway Books, 2020.

Kibert, Charles. *Sustainable Construction: Green Building Design and Delivery* 5th Edition. Hoboken, NJ: Wiley, 2022.

Lussier, Georgian, and William Lussier. *Building Success in the Trades: Career Advice for Students, Parents, Educators and Experienced Tradespeople*. Independently Published, 2019.

Mason, P.D. *Apprenticeship Career Planning for Teens*. Plymouth, MN: SugarDog Publishing, 2023.

Morkes, Andrew. *Construction & Building* Inspector. Broomall, PA: Mason Crest, 2019.

Santore, Marcia. *Plumbers: A Practical Career Guide*. Lanham, MD: Rowman & Littlefield, 2020.

Skourtis, Pantelis. *Design a House with AutoCAD Architecture*. Independently Published, 2021.

Willkens, Danielle. *Architecture for Teens: A Beginner's Book for Aspiring Architects*. Emeryville, CA: Rockridge Press, 2021.

INDEX

A

B

C

D

E

F

G

H

I

ABOUT THE AUTHOR

KATHLEEN A. KLATTE is the author of many nonfiction books for children and teens. Topics range from animals and nature to constitutional law to unusual career choices. She lives in New York with one cat and far too many books and Legos.

PHOTO CREDITS

Photo credits: Cover, p. 1 GBJSTOCK/Shutterstock.com; pp. 1, 3-96 Merydolla/Shutterstock.com; p. 5 AUUSanAKUL/Shutterstock.com; p. 6 Sayan Puangkham/Shutterstock.com; p. 7 Suzanne Tucker/Shutterstock.com; p. 9 Quality Stock Arts/Shutterstock.com; p. 14 PaeGAG/Shutterstock.com; p. 18 Monkey Business Images/Shutterstock.com; p. 19 Daniel Reiner/Shutterstock.com; p. 21 Irene Miller/Shutterstock.com; p. 22 Dmitry Kalinovsky/Shutterstock.com; p. 24 travis houston/Shutterstock.com; p. 26 Ekaterina_Minaeva/Shutterstock.com; p. 28 P.KASIPAT/Shutterstock.com; p. 29 trabantos/Shutterstock.com; p. 30 HacKLeR/Shutterstock.com; p. 31 Parilov/Shutterstock.com; p. 32 MexChriss/Shutterstock.com; p. 35 Irina_Kulikova/Shutterstock.com; p. 37 FotoDuets/Shutterstock.com; p. 39 a katz/Shutterstock.com; p. 43 LETOPISEC/Shutterstock.com; p. 45 rawf8/Shutterstock.com; p. 46 Gorodenkoff/Shutterstock.com; p. 49 Phoderstock/Shutterstock.com; p. 51 edchechine/Shutterstock.com; p. 53 Pearl PhotoPix/Shutterstock.com; p. 56 ANNVIPS/Shutterstock.com; p. 58 Stock-Asso/Shutterstock.com; p. 61 canadastock/Shutterstock.com; p. 63 kazoka/Shutterstock.com; p. 64 DimiSotirov/Shutterstock.com; p. 67 Robert Kneschke/Shutterstock.com; p. 69 Stock Creative/Shutterstock.com; p. 70 Bannafarsai_Stock/Shutterstock.com; p. 72 Gorodenkoff/Shutterstock.com; p. 73 CebotariN/Shutterstock.com; p. 75 Daniel M Ernst/Shutterstock.com; p. 78 PeopleImages.com - Yuri A./Shutterstock.com; p. 79 Drazen Zigic/Shutterstock.com; p. 80 ChameleonsEye/Shutterstock.com; p. 81 Panumas Yanuthai/Shutterstock.com; p. 83 Wandering views/Shutterstock.com.